ASPECT BOOKS:
EASY MILLIONAIRE MATH
CRACKING THE CODE TO EXPONENTIAL GROWTH AND SUCCESS
RÓBERT GERÉB

Aspect:
1. Favorable opportunity. A favorable condition inherent in a situation that enables an action or activity.
2. Mental attitude; a perception stemming from a characteristic way of thinking of a person or community, based on which they evaluate, view, or form opinions about themselves, other people, matters, events, phenomena, and things of the world and life; point of view.

© Róbert Geréb 2024
All rights reserved!

"EFFICIENCY CONSULTANT USING ADVANCED ASSISTIVE SOFTWARE SOLUTIONS TO FINE-TUNE COMPANY OPERATIONS, RESULTING IN A MORE UNIFIED, COMPETENT, AND SMOOTHLY RUNNING ORGANISATION."

Róbert Geréb
www.gerebrobert.com

To my loving Melissa!

Thank you for your unwavering love, support, and dedication. Your presence in my life has been a constant source of strength, comfort, and inspiration. Through the ups and downs, the challenges and the triumphs, you have always been by my side, offering your love, wisdom, and encouragement.

Your belief in me and my dreams has been a driving force behind my success, and I couldn't have achieved any of it without you.

Spread your word!

Welcome to this journey of unlocking financial freedom. If you find the ideas in this book inspiring or valuable, I'd be deeply grateful if you could take a moment to share your thoughts with others by leaving a review on Amazon or by emailing me at consulting@gerebrobert.com. Your feedback helps more readers discover these insights and take the first step toward achieving their dreams. Let's make an impact together!

The reason why	1
Prologue	3
The Millionaire Mindset	6
Breaking Free	9
The Power of Leveraged Products	12
Reverse-Engineering	15
The Power of Thought	18
Millionaire Math	21
Scaling Value	26
Doing the Work Once	30
Choosing the Right Product/Service	33
Building Trust and Demonstrating Value	36
Putting It All Together	40
Extra content - 50 ideas	43
Epilogue	46
My services for your wealth	50

THE REASON WHY

What do you think makes one person more successful than another?

Let's see how the dictionary defines the word "successful": "A person, process, change, period, or thing that has achieved the desired result, reaching the state, situation, or effect set as a goal." Now, please read it again and make sure you understand every single word of this very important definition! Ask yourself honestly and courageously, what is your goal? What do you need to do to achieve it? What would be the ideal state for you?

YOU MUST UNDERSTAND THAT WHEN YOU WANT A MORE DIGNIFIED WORKPLACE OR BETTER RESULTS, YOU WILL NEED NEW SKILLS AND A NEW WAY OF THINKING TO REPLACE THE OLD ONES.

I have met many successful people and consider myself fortunate to count some of them as acquaintances and friends. They have one thing in common: THEY ARE CONSTANTLY LEARNING. I read somewhere that successful people are the apostles of lifelong learning. And this is no coincidence! Just think about how many new or unusual tasks you have to solve every day from birth onwards. From school to work to your private life, everything presents serious challenges, and it makes a huge difference how you go through them. Successful people CONTINUOUSLY educate themselves to overcome difficulties on the way to their goals, which is why they achieve better results than others. Out of "forgivable selfishness," successful individuals seek the company of those smarter than themselves to gain information that makes the other person even more successful than they are. Successful people think in terms of systems and the big picture, look for connections, and harness these to serve their own goals. They read a lot, learn consciously, and do not allow themselves to be held back by any learning aversion instilled in them due to the shortcomings of the school system or other circumstances. Believe me, learning and developing as an adult is a tremendous experience and extremely useful! It saddens me when I hear, "I've learned enough; I couldn't wait for it to be over!" Such a person will probably never be able to progress from one level to the next, drifting aimlessly and living their entire life in a trap of their own making... I ask again: What is your goal, and how do you want to get there? Are you educating yourself, or are you just daydreaming?

    Dear reader! You probably aren't holding this book by chance, and you want to do something to make things better for you and live a life more worthy of you through learning. And I want to give you immediately applicable knowledge. I wish you a pleasant and useful read!

Róbert Geréb

PROLOGUE

Unlocking the Path to Financial Freedom

In a world where financial stability and personal fulfillment often seem like distant dreams, it's time to ask ourselves some crucial questions. Why is wealth necessary? Why should you act now? And why is achieving financial success easier than you might think?

Wealth is not just about accumulating money; it's about gaining the freedom to live life on your own terms. It's about having the resources to pursue your passions, support your loved ones, and make a positive impact on the world. Without financial stability, we often find ourselves trapped in a cycle of endless work and stress, unable to truly enjoy the fruits of our labor.

But why is it so important to act now? The truth is, the earlier you start your journey towards financial freedom, the more time you have to compound your efforts and reap the rewards. Procrastination is the enemy of progress, and every day you delay is a day you lose in terms of potential growth and opportunities. The world is constantly evolving, and those who adapt and take action are the ones who will thrive in the face of change.

Now, you might be thinking, "But isn't achieving financial success incredibly difficult?" The answer is no, it doesn't have to be. In fact, with the right mindset, strategies, and tools, building wealth can be far easier than you ever imagined. This book is designed to demystify the path to financial freedom and provide you with a clear, actionable blueprint for success.

Throughout the following chapters, we'll explore the key principles and techniques that have helped countless individuals transform their financial lives. *We'll start by examining the importance of setting a clear, ambitious goal – whether it's* earning a million dollars or achieving a specific level of financial independence. By defining your target and breaking it down into smaller, manageable milestones, you'll be able to stay motivated and focused on your journey.

Next, we'll dive into the power of creating leveraged income streams. You'll learn how to disconnect your time from your income by developing products or services that can be sold repeatedly with minimal effort. By embracing this mindset and focusing on building scalable assets, you'll be able to break free from the limitations of trading your time for money.

But creating a valuable product is just the beginning. To truly achieve financial success, you need to understand how to scale your efforts and maximize your impact. We'll explore the concept of **"millionaire math"** and show you how increasing the perceived value of your offerings can help you reach your goals faster. You'll discover how to transform a simple product into a high-ticket coaching program or mentorship, enabling you to serve more people while generating greater income.

Of course, none of this is possible without the right mindset. Throughout the book, we'll emphasize the importance of cultivating an abundance mentality and focusing on the opportunities rather than the obstacles. You'll learn how to reframe limiting beliefs and ask empowering questions that unlock your full potential.

As you embark on this transformative journey, remember that you're not alone. Countless individuals have walked this path before you and achieved remarkable success. By learning from their experiences and applying the principles outlined in this book, you too can join the ranks of those who have built a life of financial freedom and fulfillment.

So, are you ready to take control of your financial destiny? Are you prepared to embrace the mindset and strategies that will unlock a world of limitless possibilities? If so, then let's dive in and begin your journey towards a life of wealth, abundance, and true fulfillment.

Remember, the path to financial freedom is not a sprint, but a marathon. It requires patience, persistence, and a willingness to learn and grow. But with the right tools, mindset, and support, you can achieve things you never thought possible.

Get ready to challenge your beliefs, expand your horizons, and embark on a transformative journey towards the life you've always dreamed of.

The time to act is now – let's get started!

1
THE MILLIONAIRE MINDSET
Questions to unlock Your potential

Have you ever wondered what it takes to become a millionaire? Is it pure luck, hard work, or a combination of both? What if I told you that the key to unlocking your millionaire potential lies in your mindset and approach to generating wealth? In this book, we'll explore the fundamental principles that can transform your financial future and set you on the path to becoming a millionaire.

But before we dive into the answers, let's start by asking some essential questions:

A. Are you tired of trading your time for money, feeling like you're stuck in a never-ending cycle of working harder but not seeing significant financial growth?

B. Do you believe that your income is limited by the number of hours you can work in a day, week, or month?

C. Have you ever thought about creating a product or service that you can sell repeatedly, without having to start from scratch each time?

D. What if you could disconnect your revenue generation from your time and create a scalable, leveraged business that allows you to earn money even while you sleep?

E. Are you ready to embrace a millionaire mindset and learn the strategies that can help you achieve your financial goals faster than you ever thought possible?

If you answered "yes" to any of these questions, then this book is for you. Throughout the following chapters, we'll explore the answers to these questions and provide you with a roadmap to building sustainable wealth.

We'll challenge the traditional notion of trading time for money and introduce you to the concept of creating leveraged products that can generate income without requiring your constant presence. *You'll learn how to identify and develop a product or service that you can create once and sell countless times, allowing you to scale your business and reach your financial goals more efficiently.*

But how do you determine the right price for your product? How many customers do you need to reach your million-dollar target? And what if the number of customers you need feels overwhelming or unattainable? We'll tackle these questions head-on and introduce you to the power of "millionaire math," a game-changing approach that can help you reduce the number of customers you need by increasing the value and price of your offering.

You'll discover how to transform a simple e-book into a high-value coaching program or mentorship experience, allowing you to charge premium prices while providing unparalleled value to your customers. By focusing on delivering real, impactful results, you'll be able to justify higher price points and attract a loyal customer base that appreciates the transformative power of your product or service.

But the journey to becoming a millionaire isn't just about the tactics and strategies; it's also about adopting the right mindset. We'll explore the importance of asking empowering questions, focusing on solutions rather than limitations, and embracing the concept of leverage to create exponential growth in your business and personal wealth.

Are you ready to embark on this transformative journey and unlock your millionaire potential? In the following chapters, we'll provide you with the tools, insights, and inspiration you need to start building your leveraged business and creating the financial future you've always dreamed of.

So, let's dive in and start asking the right questions, challenging our limiting beliefs, and embracing the millionaire mindset that will set us on the path to success.

Your journey to financial freedom starts now.

2
BREAKING FREE
...from the time-money trap

In our society, most people are taught to believe that the path to financial success lies in trading their time for money. From a young age, we're conditioned to think that the key to earning a living is to find a job, work hard, and climb the corporate ladder. We're told that if we want to increase our income, we need to work longer hours, take on more responsibilities, or seek out higher-paying positions. But what if this traditional approach to generating wealth is actually holding us back from achieving our full financial potential?

The truth is, if you want to build unlimited wealth and create true financial freedom, you must disconnect your revenue generation from your time. This means breaking free from the mindset that your income is directly tied to the number of hours you work in a day, week, or month. It means recognizing that trading time for money is a limiting belief that will keep you stuck in a cycle of working harder but not necessarily smarter.

Think about it this way: if your income is solely dependent on the hours you put in, there will always be a ceiling on how much you can earn. No matter how hard you work or how much you excel in your job, there are only 24 hours in a day, and you can't create more time. This means that your earning potential is inherently limited by the finite nature of time itself.

Moreover, when you're trapped in the time-money paradigm, you're essentially selling your most precious resource—your time—for a fixed price. You're putting a dollar value on every hour of your life, and in doing so, you're limiting your ability to create true wealth and freedom. You're also sacrificing the opportunity to pursue your passions, spend time with loved ones, or enjoy the fruits of your labor because you're constantly trading your time for a paycheck.

So, how do you break free from this limiting mindset and start generating wealth that isn't tied to your time? The key is to shift your focus from active income (trading time for money) to passive income (earning money without requiring your constant presence or effort). This means creating leveraged products or services that can generate revenue even while you sleep, allowing you to scale your income without necessarily scaling your time investment.

One powerful way to create passive income is by developing a product that you can create once and sell repeatedly. This could be an e-book, an online course, a software program, or any other type of digital or physical product that provides value to your target audience. By pouring your time and effort into creating a high-quality, valuable product upfront, you can then sell it to an unlimited number of customers without having to recreate it each time.

The beauty of this approach is that it allows you to disconnect your revenue generation from your time in a scalable way. Instead of trading hours for dollars, you're leveraging your knowledge, skills, and expertise to create an asset that can continue to generate income long after you've finished creating it. This means that you can earn money while you're sleeping, traveling, or pursuing other passions, without being tied to a specific schedule or location.

Of course, creating a successful product requires upfront time and effort, and it may take some trial and error to find the right offering that resonates with your target market. But the key is to embrace the mindset that your time is a valuable resource that shouldn't be traded for a fixed price and to start exploring ways to create leveraged income streams that can grow and scale over time.

Another way to disconnect your revenue generation from your time is by building a team or outsourcing certain tasks and responsibilities. By delegating work to others and leveraging their skills and expertise, you can free up your own time to focus on high-level strategy, business development, and other activities that generate the most value for your business. This allows you to scale your impact and revenue without necessarily scaling your personal time investment.

Ultimately, breaking free from the time-money trap requires a shift in mindset and a willingness to think differently about how you generate wealth. It means recognizing that your time is your most precious resource and that trading it for a fixed price will always limit your potential for growth and success. By embracing the concept of passive income, creating leveraged products and services, and building a team to support your vision, you can start to disconnect your revenue generation from your time and unlock a world of unlimited financial potential.

But this shift in mindset isn't always easy, and it may require you to challenge deeply ingrained beliefs about work, money, and success. You may face resistance from friends, family, or colleagues who are still trapped in the time-money paradigm, and you may encounter setbacks or obstacles along the way. But by staying focused on your vision, surrounding yourself with like-minded individuals, and taking consistent action towards your goals, you can break free from the limitations of trading time for money and start building the financial future you've always dreamed of.

In the following chapters, we'll explore specific strategies and tactics for creating leveraged income streams, developing high-value products and services, and building a business that generates wealth on autopilot. But remember, the journey to financial freedom starts with a simple shift in mindset: recognizing that your time is your most valuable asset and that trading it for a fixed price will always limit your potential for growth and success.

By embracing this truth and taking action to disconnect your revenue generation from your time, you'll be well on your way to achieving the wealth, freedom, and fulfillment you deserve.

3
THE POWER OF LEVERAGED PRODUCTS

Building it once, selling unlimited times

In the previous chapter, we explored the importance of disconnecting your revenue generation from your time and embracing the concept of passive income. One of the most powerful ways to create passive income is by developing a product that you can build once and sell an unlimited number of times. This approach allows you to leverage your time, skills, and expertise to create an asset that can generate ongoing revenue without requiring your constant presence or effort.

The beauty of creating a leveraged product is that it allows you to scale your income without necessarily scaling your time investment. Once you've put in the initial effort to create a high-quality, valuable product, you can continue to sell it to new customers without having to start from scratch each time. This means that you can earn money while you sleep, travel, or pursue other passions, without being tied to a specific schedule or location.

So, what types of products can you create that fit this model of "build once, sell unlimited times"? The possibilities are endless, but here are a few examples of leveraged products that can be sold online:

- **E-books and digital guides:** If you have expertise in a particular subject or niche, consider creating an e-book or digital guide that shares your knowledge and insights with others. You can write the content once, format it into a professional-looking PDF or e-book format, and sell it through your website, online

marketplaces, or even through affiliate partnerships with other businesses in your industry.
- **Online courses and training programs:** Another way to package your knowledge and expertise is by creating an online course or training program. You can use video lessons, worksheets, quizzes, and other interactive elements to teach a specific skill or topic, and sell access to the course through a learning management system or online course platform. Once you've created the course content, you can continue to sell it to new students without having to recreate it each time.
- **Software and digital tools:** If you have programming or development skills, consider creating a software program, app, or digital tool that solves a specific problem or meets a particular need in your target market. You can sell licenses or subscriptions to the software, or offer it as a one-time purchase. Once you've built the initial product, you can continue to sell it to new customers without having to rebuild it from scratch.
- **Templates and printables:** If you have design or creative skills, consider creating templates, printables, or other digital assets that people can use for their own projects or businesses. This could include social media templates, resume templates, wedding invitations, or any other type of customizable design asset. You can create the templates once and sell them as downloadable files through your website or online marketplaces.
- **Physical products with digital components:** While physical products may require more upfront investment and ongoing management than purely digital products, you can still leverage the power of "build once, sell unlimited times" by creating physical products with digital components. For example, you could create a planner or journal that comes with access to an online community, digital resources, or video tutorials. By offering a hybrid product that combines physical and digital elements, you can create ongoing value for your customers and generate recurring revenue.

The key to creating a successful leveraged product is to identify a specific problem, need, or desire in your target market and create a solution that provides real value and results. This means doing your research, understanding your audience, and creating a product that is high-quality, engaging, and easy to use.

It's also important to consider the marketing and distribution strategy for your product. How will you get it in front of your ideal customers? How will you price it to maximize both accessibility and profitability? Will you offer any bonuses, upsells, or cross-sells to increase the average customer value? By thinking through these questions and creating a comprehensive plan for your product launch and ongoing sales, you can set yourself up for success and create a leveraged income stream that grows over time.

Of course, creating a successful product takes time, effort, and often a bit of trial and error. You may need to iterate on your initial idea, test different marketing strategies, or refine your offering based on customer feedback. But by staying focused on your goals, putting in the work to create a truly valuable product, and consistently showing up to promote and sell it, you can build a leveraged income stream that supports your financial goals and gives you the freedom and flexibility to live life on your own terms.

In the next chapter, we'll dive deeper into the process of identifying your ideal product idea, validating it with your target market, and creating a plan to bring it to life. Whether you're starting from scratch or looking to diversify your existing income streams, the power of leveraged products is one of the most effective ways to build wealth and create true financial freedom. So let's get started!

4
REVERSE-ENGINEERING

...your million-dollar goal

In the previous chapter, we explored the power of leveraged products and how creating something once and selling it unlimited times can help you break free from the time-money trap. Now, let's take this concept a step further and see how you can apply it to achieve a specific financial goal – in this case, earning *$1,000,000*.

While a million dollars may seem like an intimidating number at first glance, breaking it down into smaller, more manageable chunks can make it feel much more attainable. Let's reverse-engineer this goal and see how you can reach it by creating a simple, leveraged product like an e-book.

Step 1: Determine your product price and target customer base
For the sake of this example, let's say you create an e-book and price it at $20. This is a reasonable price point for an e-book that provides valuable information and insights to your target audience. To reach your million-dollar goal, you would need to sell this e-book to 50,000 customers. While this may seem like a large number, remember that you're not limited by geography or time when selling a digital product online.

Step 2: Break down your goal into smaller milestones Selling 50,000 copies of your e-book may feel overwhelming at first, but breaking this goal down into smaller milestones can make it feel more manageable. For example, you could set a goal to sell 1,000 copies in your first month, 2,500 copies in your second month, and so on. By setting smaller, incremental goals, you can track your progress and make adjustments to your marketing and sales strategies as needed.

Step 3: Create a high-quality, valuable product to sell 50,000 copies of your e-book, you need to create a product that provides real value and solves a specific problem or meets a particular need for your target audience. This means investing time and effort into researching your topic, organizing your content in a clear and engaging way, and designing an attractive and professional-looking e-book. Don't skimp on quality – the more value you provide, the easier it will be to market and sell your product.

Step 4: Develop a comprehensive marketing strategy Creating a great product is only half the battle – you also need to get it in front of the right people. This means developing a comprehensive marketing strategy that includes elements like content marketing, social media marketing, email marketing, and paid advertising. By creating valuable content that attracts and engages your target audience, building relationships with influencers and partners in your niche, and leveraging paid advertising to reach new customers, you can steadily grow your customer base and work towards your million-dollar goal.

Step 5: Optimize your sales funnel and customer experience As you start to generate sales and build momentum, it's important to optimize your sales funnel and customer experience to maximize your revenue and minimize churn. This means creating a seamless purchasing process, delivering your product in a timely and professional manner, and providing excellent customer support to ensure that your buyers are satisfied with their purchase. You may also want to consider offering upsells, cross-sells, or subscription options to increase the lifetime value of each customer.

Step 6: Reinvest your profits and scale your business As you start to generate revenue from your e-book sales, it's important to reinvest some of your profits back into your business. This could mean hiring a virtual assistant to help with customer support, investing in new marketing channels or tools, or even creating additional products to sell to your existing customer base. By continually reinvesting in your business and looking for ways to scale and grow, you can work towards your million-dollar goal and build a sustainable, profitable online business.

While earning a million dollars from a single e-book may seem like a daunting task, breaking it down into smaller, more manageable steps can make it feel much more achievable. By creating a high-quality product, developing a comprehensive marketing strategy, optimizing your sales funnel, and continually reinvesting in your business, you can work towards your financial goals and build a successful online business that generates passive income and gives you the freedom and flexibility to live life on your own terms.

REMEMBER, THE KEY TO SUCCESS WITH THIS MODEL IS CONSISTENCY AND PERSISTENCE.

You may not reach your million-dollar goal overnight, but by staying focused on your vision, putting in the work to create a valuable product and market it effectively, and continually iterating and improving your strategies, you can build a leveraged income stream that grows over time and helps you achieve your financial dreams.

So, whether you're creating an e-book, an online course, a software program, or any other type of leveraged product, remember that the path to a million dollars (or any other financial goal) starts with a single step. By reverse-engineering your goal, breaking it down into smaller milestones, and taking consistent action towards your vision, you can build a successful online business that generates passive income and gives you the freedom and flexibility to live life on your own terms.

5
THE POWER OF THOUGHT
Asking empowering questions

In the previous chapter, we broke down the process of reverse-engineering a million-dollar goal and explored how creating a leveraged product like an e-book can help you achieve this financial milestone. However, as you start to think about the steps involved in reaching this goal, you may find yourself facing some mental roadblocks or objections.

One of the most common objections people have when considering a goal like selling 50,000 copies of an e-book is, "I don't know how to get 50,000 customers." This is a natural thought, but it's important to recognize that it's also a disempowering one. When you focus on what you don't know or what you perceive as impossible, you limit your ability to find solutions and take action towards your goals.

As the saying goes, "If you ask disempowering questions, you cannot find empowering answers." In other words, the quality of your thoughts and the questions you ask yourself have a direct impact on your ability to achieve your goals. If you're constantly focusing on your limitations or the obstacles in your path, you'll find it much harder to make progress and reach your full potential. On the other hand, if you start asking empowering questions like, "How can I reach 50,000 customers?" you open yourself up to new possibilities and solutions. By shifting your focus from what you can't do to what you can do, you put yourself in a more proactive and resourceful state of mind.

This is where the power of thought comes into play. Your thoughts have a direct impact on your emotions, your actions, and ultimately, your results. If you're constantly thinking negative, limiting thoughts like, "I don't know how to do this," or "This is impossible," you'll find it much harder to take the necessary steps to achieve your goals.

On the other hand, if you cultivate a mindset of curiosity, possibility, and resourcefulness, you'll be much more likely to find creative solutions and take consistent action towards your goals. This means replacing disempowering questions with empowering ones, and focusing on what you can control rather than what you can't.

For example, instead of getting stuck on the question of how to get 50,000 customers, start brainstorming ways to reach more people and provide more value:

- *Could you partner with influencers or other businesses in your niche to expand your reach?*
- *Could you create a lead magnet or free resource that attracts potential customers and builds your email list?*
- *Could you invest in paid advertising or social media marketing to get your product in front of a wider audience?*

By asking these types of questions and exploring different possibilities, you'll start to generate ideas and take action towards your goals. You may not have all the answers right away, but by staying focused on what you can do and taking consistent steps forward, you'll build momentum and start to see results.

ANOTHER KEY ASPECT OF CULTIVATING AN EMPOWERING MINDSET IS FOCUSING ON THE VALUE YOU PROVIDE RATHER THAN JUST THE PRICE OF YOUR PRODUCT.

As we discussed in the previous chapter, one way to increase your revenue and reach your financial goals faster is by increasing the perceived value of your product and charging a higher price.

However, this doesn't mean simply raising your prices without justification. Instead, it means looking for ways to provide more value to your customers and create a more comprehensive and supportive experience. For example, instead of just selling an e-book, could you create a companion course or coaching program that helps customers implement the strategies and techniques you teach? Could you offer personalized support or feedback to help customers overcome challenges and achieve their goals? By focusing on providing more value and support to your customers, you can justify charging a higher price and create a more sustainable and profitable business model. This is how successful entrepreneurs and millionaires think – they focus on leverage and creating exponential value rather than just trading time for money.

Ultimately, the power of thought is about recognizing that your mindset and the questions you ask yourself have a direct impact on your ability to achieve your goals. By cultivating an empowering, resourceful, and value-driven mindset, you can overcome obstacles, generate creative solutions, and take consistent action towards your vision.

So, as you work towards your million-dollar goal and beyond, remember to focus on asking empowering questions, exploring possibilities, and providing as much value as possible to your customers. By doing so, you'll build a strong foundation for success and create a business that generates passive income and gives you the freedom and flexibility to live life on your own terms.

6
MILLIONAIRE MATH
Scaling Your impact and income

One of the most common objections people have when considering a goal like selling 50,000 copies of an e-book is, "I don't know how to get 50,000 customers." However, by shifting your mindset and focusing on what you can control, you open yourself up to new possibilities and solutions.

This is where millionaire math comes into play. Instead of getting stuck on the idea of reaching 50,000 customers, what if you could achieve your million-dollar goal with a smaller number of customers by increasing the price of your product?

For example, let's say you're selling an e-book for $20. To reach your goal of $1,000,000 in revenue, you would need to sell 50,000 copies. However, if you increase the price of your e-book to $200, you now only need to sell 5,000 copies to reach the same revenue goal.

This simple shift in pricing can have a profound impact on your business and your ability to reach your financial goals. By focusing on creating a higher-value product and charging a premium price, you can reduce the number of customers you need to reach and make your million-dollar goal feel much more attainable.

Of course, increasing your price isn't just about arbitrary numbers. To justify charging a higher price, you need to focus on providing more value to your customers. This means going beyond just selling an e-book and creating a more comprehensive and supportive experience for your buyers.

For example, instead of just selling an e-book, you could create a companion course or coaching program for $200 that helps customers implement the strategies and techniques you teach.

You could offer personalized support, feedback, or accountability for $2,000 to help customers overcome challenges and achieve their goals. By providing a higher level of value and support, you can justify charging a premium price and create a more engaged and loyal customer base. In this case you need just 500 customers to reach te $1,000,00 goal.

This is how successful entrepreneurs and millionaires think — they focus on leverage and creating exponential value rather than just trading time for money. By doing the work once to create a high-value product and then scaling it to reach a larger audience, you can create a business that generates passive income and allows you to make a significant impact in your industry.

The power of millionaire math is that it allows you to shift your focus from the number of customers you need to reach to the value you provide and the impact you can make.

INSTEAD OF GETTING STUCK ON THE IDEA OF REACHING 50,000 CUSTOMERS, YOU CAN FOCUS ON CREATING A PRODUCT THAT IS SO VALUABLE AND TRANSFORMATIVE THAT CUSTOMERS ARE WILLING TO PAY A PREMIUM PRICE FOR IT.

This shift in thinking can be a huge leap forward for your business and your personal growth. By focusing on creating exponential value and scaling your impact, you open yourself up to new opportunities and possibilities. You start to see your business not just as a way to make money, but as a vehicle for making a difference in people's lives and leaving a lasting legacy.

So, as you work towards your million-dollar goal, remember that the key to success is not just in the numbers, but in the value you provide and the impact you make. By focusing on creating a high-value product, providing exceptional support and service, and scaling your business through leverage and automation, you can achieve your financial goals while also making a meaningful difference in the world.

MILLIONAIRE MATH IS NOT JUST ABOUT THE NUMBERS – IT'S ABOUT THE MINDSET AND THE STRATEGIES YOU USE TO CREATE EXPONENTIAL GROWTH AND IMPACT. BY SHIFTING YOUR FOCUS FROM LIMITATIONS TO POSSIBILITIES, AND BY CONTINUALLY STRIVING TO PROVIDE MORE VALUE AND SUPPORT TO YOUR CUSTOMERS, YOU CAN BUILD A BUSINESS THAT NOT ONLY GENERATES PASSIVE INCOME, BUT ALSO ALLOWS YOU TO LIVE A LIFE OF PURPOSE, PASSION, AND ABUNDANCE.

The "millionaire math" concept in your text breaks down the process of earning $1,000,000 by reverse-engineering income goals. Here's how it works with real numbers:

STEP 1: THE GOAL

We aim to earn $1,000,000 by selling a product that can be created once and sold multiple times (like an e-book, course, or coaching program).

STEP 2: BASIC CALCULATION

If you sell a product priced at $20, you need 50,000 customers to reach $1,000,000:

$$\text{Calculation: } \frac{1,000,000}{20} = 50,000$$

STEP 3: INCREASING PRICE TO REDUCE CUSTOMERS

By increasing the product price, you reduce the number of customers required to hit the $1,000,000 mark. Here's the breakdown:

1. **$200 Product:**

$$\text{Customers needed: } \frac{1,000,000}{200} = 5,000$$

You create a premium product, like a live coaching community.

2. **$2,000 Product:**

$$\text{Customers needed: } \frac{1,000,000}{2,000} = 500$$

This could be a high-ticket mentorship program where you provide one-on-one guidance.

STEP 4: PRICING STRATEGY

Let's assume you evolve your product over time:
1. Start with an e-book ($20): Sell 1,000 copies to earn $20,000.

2. Upgrade to live coaching ($200): Get 250 customers to earn $50,000.
3. Launch a mentorship program ($2,000): Find 150 clients to earn $300,000.

Total revenue so far: $370,000.

Repeat or scale each step to hit the $1,000,000 target.

STEP 5: BREAK DOWN CUSTOMER ACQUISITION

Now, let's say you aim to sell 1,000 units of a $1,000 product. To achieve this:
- Target 83 customers per month (1,000 ÷ 12 months).
- Attract 3 customers per day using marketing (e.g., ads, content creation, social media).
- If your product is priced at $500, you'll need:

$$\frac{2,000}{12} = 167 \text{ customers per month (or 6/day)}.$$

THE TAKEAWAY

By focusing on fewer high-value customers, you simplify your path to $1,000,000. As you refine your product and marketing strategy, the focus should be on increasing perceived value and pricing.

7
SCALING VALUE

From e-book to high-ticket mentorship

However, increasing your price isn't just about picking a higher number – it's about providing more value to your customers and creating a more transformative experience. Let's say you start by creating an e-book that teaches a specific skill or strategy. You price it at $20 and start promoting it to your audience. As you make sales and gather feedback, you realize that many of your customers are looking for more support and guidance in implementing the concepts you teach.

This is where you can start to think about scaling the value of your product. Instead of just selling an e-book, what if you could create a coaching program that provides live guidance and support to your customers? You could offer weekly group coaching calls, personalized feedback on assignments, and a private community where customers can connect and support each other.

By offering this higher level of support and accountability, you can justify charging a higher price for your program. Instead of $20 for an e-book, you might charge $200 for a comprehensive coaching experience. While this might seem like a big jump in price, remember that customers are willing to pay for results. If your coaching program can help them achieve their goals faster and with more confidence, they'll gladly invest in the experience.

For example, let's say your e-book teaches people how to start a successful online business. By creating a coaching program, you could provide live guidance on choosing a niche, creating a website, and launching a product. You could offer personalized feedback on your customers' business ideas and help them troubleshoot challenges along the way. By providing this level of support, you can help your customers achieve real, tangible results – and that's something they'll be happy to pay for.

But what if you want to take it even further? After successfully selling your coaching program at $200, you might start to think about how you can provide even more value to your customers. This is where high-ticket mentorship comes in.

At this level, you're not just selling knowledge or support – you're offering a transformative, one-on-one experience that helps your customers achieve their biggest goals and dreams. You might offer a year-long mentorship program that includes weekly one-on-one calls, personalized strategy sessions, and unlimited email support. You could even offer in-person retreats or workshops where customers can connect with you and other high-level entrepreneurs.

By offering this level of personalized attention and support, you can justify charging premium prices for your mentorship program. Instead of $200 for a group coaching experience, you might charge $2,000 or even $5,000 for a high-level mentorship package. While this might seem like a lot of money, remember that you're not just selling information – you're selling transformation.

$20 X 50,000 CUSTOMERS = $1,000,000
$200 X 5,000 CUSTOMERS = $1,000,000
$5,000 X 200 CUSTOMERS = $1,000,000
$12,000 X 84 CUSTOMERS = $1,000,000

For example, let's say you're a successful real estate investor who has built a multi-million dollar portfolio. You could create a high-ticket mentorship program that teaches aspiring investors how to find, finance, and manage profitable rental properties. You might offer one-on-one coaching calls to help your students create a personalized investment strategy, provide feedback on their deals, and help them navigate challenges along the way. You could even offer in-person workshops where students can visit your properties and learn from your team.

By offering this level of personalized attention and support, you can help your students achieve life-changing results – and that's something they'll be willing to invest in. When you're selling transformation and not just information, you can charge premium prices and still provide incredible value to your customers.

Of course, creating a high-ticket mentorship program requires a significant investment of time and energy on your part. You'll need to create a comprehensive curriculum, develop a strong personal brand, and provide an exceptional level of service to your customers. But by focusing on providing real, transformative results, you can build a loyal customer base and create a business that generates significant revenue with a smaller number of clients.

As you think about scaling the value of your own products and services, consider how you can provide more support, guidance, and transformation to your customers. Can you create a group coaching program that helps them implement your strategies and achieve their goals? Can you offer one-on-one mentorship that provides personalized attention and support? By continually looking for ways to provide more value and impact, you can create a business that not only generates wealth but also changes lives.

But what if you're just starting out and don't have a lot of experience or expertise to share? How can you create a high-value product or service when you're still learning and growing yourself? This is a common challenge for many entrepreneurs –

and it's one we'll explore in the next chapter. Stay tuned to learn how you can leverage your unique strengths and experiences to create a valuable offering, even if you're not an expert (yet).

8
DOING THE WORK ONCE

...and scaling to exponential returns

By offering more support, guidance, and transformation to your customers, you can justify charging premium prices and create a more impactful and profitable business.

But here's the key point to remember: as you scale the value of your offering, the core product itself doesn't necessarily need to change. What changes is the perceived value and the level of support you provide to your customers.

This is where the power of leverage comes in. Leverage is all about doing the work once and then scaling it to create exponential returns. Instead of trading your time for money and starting from scratch with each new customer, you create a valuable asset that can be sold over and over again.

Let's go back to the example of creating an e-book. Once you've written and designed your e-book, you can sell it an unlimited number of times without having to create it from scratch each time. You might spend 100 hours creating the e-book, but you can sell it to 1,000 customers or 10,000 customers without spending another 100 hours each time.

This is the power of leverage – you do the work once, and then you scale it to create exponential returns. And as you scale the value of your offering by providing more support and guidance to your customers, you can increase your prices and create even more leverage.

For example, let's say you create an online course that teaches people how to start a successful freelance business. You spend several months creating the course content, recording videos, and designing worksheets and assignments. Once the course is created, you can sell it over and over again to an unlimited number of students.

But what if you want to provide more value to your students and justify charging a higher price? You could offer group coaching calls where students can ask questions and get personalized feedback. You could provide templates, scripts, and other resources to help them implement what they've learned. You could even offer a done-for-you service where you help them land their first client or create their website.

By providing these additional levels of support and service, you can increase the perceived value of your course and charge a premium price. But here's the key: you're not starting from scratch each time. You're leveraging the work you've already done to create the course content and materials, and then scaling it to provide more value to your customers.

Another example of leverage is creating a physical product that can be manufactured and sold at scale. Let's say you create a line of eco-friendly cleaning products. You spend time researching and developing the formulas, designing the packaging, and finding a manufacturer. Once you have your product line created, you can sell it over and over again to an unlimited number of customers.

But again, you can scale the value of your offering by providing more support and education to your customers. You could create a series of videos that teach people how to use your products effectively and create a cleaner, healthier home. You could offer a subscription service where customers receive a new product each month along with tips and resources for living a more sustainable lifestyle. By providing this additional value and support, you can justify charging a higher price for your products and create even more leverage.

The power of leverage is that it allows you to create exponential returns on your time and effort. Instead of trading hours for dollars and starting from scratch with each new customer, you create valuable assets that can be sold over and over again. And by continually looking for ways to scale the value of your offering and provide more support and transformation to your customers, you can create a business that generates significant wealth and impact.

Of course, creating leverage in your business requires a shift in mindset. Instead of thinking about how to make a quick sale or trade your time for money, you need to think about how to create long-term value and scale your impact. This means investing time and resources into creating high-quality products, building relationships with your customers, and continually improving and innovating your offerings.

But when you embrace the power of leverage and focus on scaling your value, the potential for growth and impact is truly unlimited. By doing the work once and creating exponential returns, you can build a business that not only generates wealth but also makes a meaningful difference in the lives of your customers and the world around you.

So as you think about your own business and how you can create more leverage, ask yourself: how can I create valuable assets that can be sold over and over again? How can I scale the value of my offering by providing more support, guidance, and transformation to my customers? And how can I continually improve and innovate my products and services to create even more impact and exponential returns?

By focusing on these key principles and embracing the power of leverage, you can build a business that not only achieves your financial goals but also creates a lasting legacy of value and impact. And that's the true definition of success – not just in business, but in life as well.

9
CHOOSING THE RIGHT PRODUCT/SERVICE

And start selling it

When it comes to creating a leveraged product that can help you achieve financial freedom and build a million-dollar business, one of the most crucial decisions you'll make is choosing the right product to focus on. The key to success lies in selecting a product that aligns with your skills, knowledge, and passion, allowing you to provide genuine value to your customers.

Many people often find themselves stuck at this stage, wondering what kind of product they should create. They may feel overwhelmed by the countless options available or doubt their ability to offer something truly valuable. However, the truth is that the best leveraged product is one that leverages your unique strengths and expertise.

No matter what your background or experience level, you have a wealth of knowledge and skills that can be transformed into a valuable product. Whether you're a talented writer, a skilled programmer, a knowledgeable coach, or an expert in a specific industry, you have the potential to create a product that resonates with your target audience.

One of the most important things to remember is that your product doesn't have to be groundbreaking or revolutionary. In fact, some of the most successful leveraged products are based on simple, everyday topics that people are eager to learn about. The key is to provide a fresh perspective, actionable insights, and genuine value that helps your customers achieve their goals or solve their problems.

For example, if you're a skilled writer with a passion for personal development, you could create an e-book or course that teaches people how to build self-confidence, overcome procrastination, or improve their relationships. Even if there are already countless books and courses on these topics, your unique voice, experiences, and insights can make your product stand out and resonate with your target audience.

Similarly, if you're a talented software developer, you could create a tool or application that simplifies a common task, automates a tedious process, or provides a valuable service to businesses or individuals. Your software doesn't have to be a complex, enterprise-level solution; even a simple, well-designed tool that solves a specific problem can be incredibly valuable to your customers.

The beauty of leveraged products is that they allow you to package your knowledge and skills into a format that can be easily shared and accessed by a wide audience. Whether you choose to create an e-book, a course, a software program, or any other type of product, the key is to focus on providing real value and solving genuine problems for your customers.

When choosing your leveraged product, it's essential to consider your target audience and their specific needs, challenges, and desires. Take the time to research your market, identify the gaps or opportunities, and create a product that addresses those needs in a unique and valuable way.

Remember, there is no such thing as a topic that is too simple or too "low-end" to create a successful leveraged product around. Some of the most profitable products are based on seemingly basic topics that people are eager to learn about, such as cooking, gardening, personal finance, or health and wellness.

The key is to approach your chosen topic with passion, expertise, and a commitment to providing genuine value to your customers. By focusing on your strengths, leveraging your knowledge and skills, and creating a product that solves real problems or helps people achieve their goals, you can build a successful and sustainable business around your leveraged product.

Another crucial aspect to consider when creating your leveraged product is **pricing**. Determining the right price for your product can be a challenging task, and it often requires some investigation and experimentation. Don't be afraid to test different price points and see how your target audience responds. Keep in mind that the perceived value of your product plays a significant role in how much people are willing to pay for it.

If you find that your first leveraged product isn't selling as well as you hoped, don't get discouraged. Instead, take it as an opportunity to learn, adapt, and try again. Analyze the feedback you receive from your customers, identify areas for improvement, and consider creating a different product that better resonates with your target audience.

Remember, success rarely comes overnight, and building a million-dollar business takes time, effort, and perseverance. By staying committed to providing value, continuously learning and improving, and being willing to experiment with different products and strategies, you can ultimately find the right leveraged product that helps you achieve your financial goals and make a positive impact on the lives of others.

As you embark on this journey of creating your own leveraged product, remember to stay true to yourself and your unique talents. Don't be afraid to explore different ideas, test your assumptions, and refine your product based on feedback from your customers. With persistence, dedication, and a commitment to providing real value, you can create a leveraged product that not only helps you achieve your financial goals but also makes a positive impact on the lives of others.

10
BUILDING TRUST AND DEMONSTRATING VALUE

The key to scalable wealth

To truly create scalable wealth, you need to focus on building trust and demonstrating value at every level of your offering. When you're first starting out, you might offer a low-priced product or service to attract customers and build trust. This could be a $20 e-book, a $50 course, or a $100 consulting session. At this level, you're focusing on providing value and establishing yourself as an expert in your field.

As you build trust and demonstrate the value of your offering, you can start to scale up to higher-priced products and services. This is where coaching and mentorship come in. By providing personalized support and guidance to your customers, you can help them achieve even better results and justify charging a premium price.

Let's look at three real-world examples of how this formula can work in different domains:

Fitness and nutrition:
- $10 product: A meal planning guide with healthy recipes and grocery lists
- $90 coaching: A 12-week online fitness program with weekly check-ins and personalized meal plans
- $7,00 mentorship: A one-on-one coaching program with a certified nutritionist and personal trainer, including in-person sessions and ongoing support

Scaling opportunities: As you build trust and demonstrate results with your low-priced products and coaching programs, you can start to offer higher-priced mentorship and even retreat experiences. You could host a weekend wellness retreat where participants receive personalized nutrition and fitness plans, attend workshops and classes, and connect with like-minded individuals. By providing a transformative experience and ongoing support, you can charge premium prices and create a scalable, high-impact business.

Personal finance and investing:
- $30 product: An e-book on budgeting and saving money
- $500 coaching: A group coaching program on investing in stocks and real estate
- $12,000 mentorship: A personalized financial planning service with a certified financial planner, including retirement planning, tax optimization, and estate planning

Scaling opportunities: As you help your clients achieve financial success and build wealth, you can start to offer even higher-priced services such as family office management and legacy planning. You could also create a mastermind group or investment club where high-net-worth individuals can connect, share ideas, and invest together. By providing exclusive access and personalized support, you can create a scalable business that generates significant wealth and impact.

Business and entrepreneurship:
- $35 product: A guide on how to start a side hustle or freelance business
- $700 coaching: A group coaching program on scaling your business and building a team
- $22,000 mentorship: A one-on-one consulting service with a successful entrepreneur, including business strategy, marketing, and operations support

Scaling opportunities: As you help your clients build and scale their businesses, you can start to offer even higher-priced services such as board advisory roles, speaking engagements, and equity partnerships. You could also create a venture capital fund or accelerator program where you invest in and mentor promising startups. By providing capital, expertise, and connections, you can create a scalable business that generates wealth and drives innovation.

In each of these examples, the key is to start by providing value and building trust with your low-priced products and services. As you demonstrate results and establish yourself as an expert, you can start to scale up to higher-priced offerings that provide even more value and support to your customers.

The beauty of this approach is that it allows you to create scalable wealth without trading your time for money. By creating valuable assets that can be sold over and over again, and by providing personalized support and guidance to your customers, you can generate exponential returns and make a meaningful impact in your industry.

Of course, building a scalable business takes time, effort, and strategic thinking. You need to continually innovate and improve your products and services, build relationships with your customers and partners, and stay focused on your long-term goals.

But when you embrace the power of building trust and demonstrating value, the opportunities for growth and impact are truly unlimited. Whether you're passionate about health and wellness, financial freedom, entrepreneurship, or any other domain, you can create a business that generates wealth, fulfillment, and positive change in the world.

So if you're wondering what kind of business to start, look for ideas that allow you to create something once and sell it multiple times. Focus on providing value and building trust with your customers, and continually look for ways to scale up and provide even more support and transformation.

The path to scalable wealth is not always easy, but it is possible. By taking action, staying focused on your goals, and continually learning and growing, you can build a business that not only achieves your financial dreams but also makes a lasting impact on the lives of others.

So what are you waiting for? Start exploring ideas, taking action, and building your own scalable business today. The world is waiting for your unique gifts and talents — and with the right mindset and strategies, there's no limit to what you can achieve.

11
PUTTING IT ALL TOGETHER

Your roadmap to financial freedom

Throughout this book, we've explored the key principles and strategies for building a successful online business and achieving your financial goals. Let's recap the main points and create a roadmap for putting these ideas into action.

First, start by setting a big, audacious goal for your business. Whether it's earning a million dollars, reaching a certain number of customers, or creating a specific level of impact, having a clear and ambitious target will help you stay motivated and focused as you build your business.

Next, break that big goal down into smaller, more manageable milestones. This could mean setting revenue targets for each month or quarter, or identifying specific numbers of customers or products sold. By creating a series of smaller, achievable goals, you'll build momentum and make consistent progress towards your larger vision.

One of the most important strategies for reaching your financial goals is to create a product that can be sold an unlimited number of times. This is the power of leveraged income – by creating something once and selling it over and over again, you can scale your revenue without linearly increasing your workload.

When creating your product, focus on providing real value and solving a specific problem or need for your target audience. Whether it's an e-book, course, software program, or physical product, make sure that it delivers tangible results and benefits to your customers. The more value you provide, the easier it will be to market and sell your product.

As you start to generate sales and revenue, look for ways to increase the perceived value of your product and create additional streams of income. This could mean adding bonuses or companion products, creating a higher-tier version of your product, or offering personalized support or coaching. By increasing the value you provide, you can justify charging higher prices and create a more profitable and sustainable business.

As you scale your business, it's important to stay true to the core principles and strategies that have brought you success. While you may need to adapt and evolve your product or marketing strategies over time, make sure that you're always focusing on providing value, building relationships with your customers, and creating leveraged income streams. Finally, don't underestimate the importance of investing in marketing and dissemination. No matter how great your product is, it won't sell itself. You need to get it in front of the right people and communicate its value effectively. This could mean investing in content marketing, social media advertising, influencer partnerships, or other strategies to reach your target audience and build your brand.

As you start to see success and reach your initial financial goals, don't be afraid to set even bigger targets for yourself. The beauty of building a leveraged income stream is that your potential for growth is virtually unlimited. By continually reinvesting in your business, improving your products and marketing strategies, and setting new goals for yourself, you can create a life of financial freedom and abundance.

So, whether you're just starting out on your entrepreneurial journey or you're looking to take your existing business to the next level, remember that success is within your reach. By following the principles and strategies outlined in this book, and by staying committed to your vision and taking consistent action, you can build a successful online business that generates passive income and allows you to live life on your own terms.

The roadmap to financial freedom is clear – set big goals, break them down into manageable steps, create valuable and leveraged products, increase your value and revenue over time, invest in marketing and dissemination, and continually strive for growth and improvement. By following these principles and staying focused on your vision, you can achieve your financial dreams and create a life of abundance and freedom. So, what are you waiting for?

GET STARTED TODAY AND TAKE THE FIRST STEP TOWARDS YOUR MILLION-DOLLAR BUSINESS!

12
EXTRA CONTENT - 50 IDEAS

Personal Development and Self-Help:
1. An e-book on overcoming procrastination and increasing productivity
2. A guided meditation course for reducing stress and anxiety
3. A video series on building self-confidence and assertiveness
4. An online workshop on developing emotional intelligence
5. A mobile app for setting and achieving personal goals

Health and Wellness:
6. A comprehensive guide to plant-based nutrition and meal planning
7. An online fitness program tailored to busy professionals
8. A video course on mindfulness and stress reduction techniques
9. An e-book on natural remedies for common health ailments
10. A mobile app for tracking sleep quality and improving sleep habits

Relationships and Dating:
11. An online course on effective communication in relationships
12. An e-book on navigating the modern dating landscape
13. A video series on building and maintaining healthy friendships
14. An online workshop on resolving conflicts in relationships
15. A mobile app for couples to strengthen their connection and intimacy

Personal Finance and Investing:
16. An e-book on creating and sticking to a budget
17. An online course on investing in the stock market for beginners

18. A video series on strategies for paying off debt and building wealth
19. An online workshop on creating multiple streams of passive income
20. A mobile app for tracking expenses and monitoring financial goals

Career Development and Entrepreneurship:
21. An e-book on transitioning to a new career or industry
22. An online course on starting and scaling a successful online business
23. A video series on developing leadership skills in the workplace
24. An online workshop on effective networking and personal branding
25. A mobile app for freelancers to manage projects and clients

Technology and Digital Skills:
26. An online course on learning to code for non-programmers
27. An e-book on digital marketing strategies for small businesses
28. A video series on mastering productivity tools like Trello and Asana
29. An online workshop on creating and editing videos using Adobe Premiere
30. A mobile app for learning and practicing a new language

Hobbies and Crafts:
31. An e-book on starting a successful vegetable garden
32. An online course on photography composition and editing techniques
33. A video series on knitting and crocheting projects for beginners
34. An online workshop on watercolor painting techniques
35. A mobile app for identifying and learning about different bird species

Parenting and Family:
36. An e-book on positive discipline strategies for parents
37. An online course on teaching children emotional regulation skills
38. A video series on engaging educational activities for toddlers
39. An online workshop on navigating the challenges of blended families
40. A mobile app for organizing family schedules and activities

Pet Care and Training:
41. An e-book on training and caring for a new puppy
42. An online course on creating a balanced diet for cats
43. A video series on teaching birds tricks and improving their behavior
44. An online workshop on creating a safe and enriching environment for reptiles
45. A mobile app for tracking pet health and medication schedules

Home Improvement and Organization:
46. An e-book on decluttering and organizing your home
47. An online course on basic home repair and maintenance skills
48. A video series on interior design principles and trends
49. An online workshop on creating a productive home office space
50. A mobile app for planning and tracking home renovation projects

Remember, these are just ideas to get you started. The key is to identify a topic that aligns with your skills, knowledge, and passion, and to create a product that provides genuine value to your target audience.

EPILOGUE
The Efficiency Consultant's impact

As we conclude this transformative journey through the pages of "Easy Millionaire Math - Cracking the code to exponential growth and success", it's important to reflect on the man behind the ideas – Róbert Geréb, the visionary Efficiency Consultant.

Róbert's passion for helping businesses and individuals achieve their full potential has been the driving force behind his work. With a unique blend of expertise in traditional business optimization and cutting-edge AI technology, he has revolutionized the way companies approach efficiency and success.

Through his consulting practice, Róbert has helped countless businesses, from small startups to large enterprises, streamline their operations, integrate AI solutions, and unlock their true potential. His clients have experienced significant improvements in productivity, profitability, and overall competitiveness, thanks to his guidance and innovative strategies.

But Róbert's impact extends far beyond his direct clients. The principles and strategies outlined in this book have resonated with readers from all walks of life, inspiring them to take control of their financial destinies and pursue their dreams with renewed vigor.

Professionals and employees have discovered the importance of continuous learning and adaptation, recognizing that in today's rapidly evolving digital landscape, staying ahead of the curve is essential for long-term success. They have embraced the mindset of efficiency and leveraged the tools and strategies presented in this book to optimize their own performance and contribute to the growth of their organizations.

Even those who have yet to embark on their entrepreneurial journey have found inspiration in Róbert's words. The idea that financial success is attainable, and that with the right mindset and strategies, anyone can build a life of abundance and fulfillment, has ignited a spark of hope and determination in countless readers.

As we look to the future, it's clear that the principles of efficiency, leverage, and AI integration will only become more relevant and important. In a world where change is the only constant, those who are able to adapt, innovate, and optimize will be the ones who thrive.

Róbert's work as an Efficiency Consultant and the ideas presented in this book provide a foundation for success in this new era. By embracing the mindset of efficiency, leveraging the power of technology, and continually striving for growth and improvement, individuals and businesses alike can navigate the challenges of the digital age and emerge stronger, more resilient, and more successful than ever before.

As you close this book and reflect on your own journey, remember that the path to financial freedom and fulfillment is not always easy, but it is always worth pursuing. With the right mindset, strategies, and support, you too can achieve the success you desire and make a lasting impact on the world around you.

Take the lessons you've learned from these pages and apply them to your own life and business. Embrace the power of efficiency, leverage, and AI, and never stop learning and growing. The future belongs to those who are willing to adapt, innovate, and optimize – and with Róbert Geréb's guidance and the principles outlined in this book, you are well on your way to unlocking your own millionaire mindset and achieving the financial freedom you deserve.

Your Opinion Matters!

Thank you for reading this book! If the concepts here resonated with you, or if you've started taking steps toward your goals, I'd love to hear your thoughts. Leaving a review on Amazon or by emailing me at consulting@gerebrobert.com not only helps me but also allows others to benefit from this knowledge. Together, we can inspire more people to build the life they deserve. Thank you for supporting the mission!

MY SERVICES FOR YOUR WEALTH

Efficiency consulting is a service that helps businesses optimize their operations, streamline processes, and maximize productivity to achieve better results with less effort. The main goal of an efficiency consultant is to identify areas of improvement within an organization and implement strategies to enhance performance, reduce costs, and increase profitability.

Here are some key aspects of efficiency consulting:

1. Process optimization: Efficiency consultants analyze existing processes and workflows to identify bottlenecks, redundancies, and inefficiencies. They then develop and implement solutions to streamline these processes, making them more efficient and cost-effective.

2. Data analysis: Consultants gather and analyze data from various sources within the organization to gain insights into performance, trends, and areas for improvement. This data-driven approach helps them make informed decisions and recommendations.

3. Technology integration: Efficiency consultants often recommend and facilitate the adoption of new technologies, such as automation tools, software solutions, and AI-powered systems, to improve efficiency and productivity.

4. Change management: Implementing new processes and technologies often requires a shift in organizational culture and employee behavior. Efficiency consultants help manage this change by communicating the benefits, providing training, and ensuring a smooth transition.

5. Continuous improvement: Efficiency consulting is an ongoing process. Consultants work with businesses to establish a culture of continuous improvement, where employees are encouraged to identify and suggest areas for optimization.

By engaging an efficiency consultant, businesses can benefit from an objective, third-party perspective on their operations, gain valuable insights, and implement strategies to improve their overall performance and competitiveness in the market.

Contact me for a consultation:
www.gerebrobert.com

© Róbert Geréb 2024
All rights reserved!

www.ingramcontent.com/pod-product-compliance
Lightning Source LLC
Chambersburg PA
CBHW070417230526
45471CB00006B/2860